91-269

MAURITIUS

MAURITIUS

MARIE BENOIT

CHELSEA HOUSE

ACKNOWLEDGEMENTS

The Author and Publishers are grateful to the following organizations and individuals for permission to reproduce copyright illustrations in this book:

Camerapix Hutchison Library Ltd; Louis Gilbert Desveaux; The Mansell Collection Ltd; The Mauritian Government Tourist Board.

Published by Chelsea House Publishers

All rights reserved

Printed and bound in Hong Kong

First printing

ISBN 1–55546–171–9

Chelsea House Publishers

Harold Steinberg, Chairman & Publisher
Susan Lusk, Vice President
A Division of Chelsea House Educational Communications, Inc.

133 Christopher Street, New York, NY 10014

345 Whitney Avenue, New Haven, CT 05510

5014 West Chester Pike, Edgemont, PA 19028

Contents

An Island of Enchantment

Distance lends enchantment and, like many small islands, Mauritius has a romantic appeal. Even today it remains (in the minds of those who have heard of it) a vague and distant place, surrounded by blue lagoons and covered by swaying palm trees.

Mauritius is indeed isolated. It forms a small speck on the map—in the Indian ocean, 800 kilometres (500 miles) east of Madagascar and 2,000 kilometres (1,250 miles) off the South African coast, lying almost on the Tropic of Capricorn. Rodrigues—a neighbouring island dependency of Mauritius — lies 580 kilometres (360 miles) to the east. Northwards, the nearest land is the Seychelles Islands which, under the British crown, were once linked with Mauritius.

Mauritius is one of the Mascarene Islands, so called after Don Pedro Mascarenhas, probably the first Portuguese navigator to visit these islands. The other two Mascarene Islands are Rodrigues and Réunion, a French department.

Mauritius is twenty degrees south of the equator and has an area of 1,865 square kilometres (720 square miles). It is sixty-one kilometres (thirty-eight miles) long and forty-seven kilometres (twenty-nine miles) wide. In this part of the world summer-time begins in December and winter-time in June.

The calm surrounding waters are clear. It is therefore possible

7

to see tropical fish, shells and other beautiful creatures. Deep-sea fishing and snorkling are favourite pastimes for Mauritians and tourists alike. Some hope to come up with treasure from ships wrecked around the coast long ago.

The climate is sub-tropical with average temperatures of about 26 degrees Celsius (79 degrees Fahrenheit) in the hottest months and 22 degrees Celsius (72 degrees Fahrenheit) in the coldest months at Port Louis, the capital. However, in the town of Curepipe, which is 560 metres (1,850 feet) above sea-level, minimum temperatures of 7 degrees Celsius (45 degrees Fahrenheit) have been recorded. The island is damp and has a fairly heavy rainfall.

Mauritius has a micro-climate so that, although it may be raining on the central plateau, the coast is warm and dry. These local variations in climate are caused by the mountain structure. The trade winds, which in days gone by used to blow the sailing-ships to and from Mauritius, ensure that the island has a relatively equable climate for a tropical place.

Mauritius is of volcanic origin, and volcanoes hurled it up from the ocean floor some seven million years ago. But volcanic activity ceased some 100,000 years ago. There are craters in Mauritius the largest of which is Trou-aux-Cerfs. On the nearby island of Réunion there is an active volcano called La Fournaise which erupts from time to time. Since the origins of both islands are similar, experts say that the craters on Mauritius may be only dormant and not dead. They could erupt in the future.

Mauritius is covered by dense forest, and surrounded by coral

Fishing in one of Mauritius' tranquil lagoons

reefs except for thirteen kilometres (eight miles). According to Charles Darwin, the famous naturalist and author, who visited the island in 1836, the reef varies in breadth between one kilometre (half a mile) and three or five kilometres (two or three miles). Coral reefs are built by tiny sea animals called polyps. Living coral is like jelly. Coral polyps like clear, warm and shallow salt water. When the polyps die, the coral becomes hard and, over the years, forms a reef. Because of the coral reef, the sea immediately around Mauritius is shallow and does not get rough except in a cyclone. It therefore forms calm lagoons where fish are plentiful though not enough for the population's needs. In those places where there is no coral reef, such as off the coast at Gris-Gris in the south of the island, the sea is usually very rough.

The coral is collected by fishermen and burned to make lime.

9

There are different types of lime. Quicklime is used in the making of sugar; slaked lime is used as a fertilizer, as well as for building purposes. The coast of Mauritius is dotted with lime-kilns in which the coral is burned. Some of these kilns are no longer used because the coral in that area has been exhausted.

The vegetation of the island is mainly tropical. Darwin found that the whole island "with its sloping border and central mountains, was adorned with an air of perfect elegance". He also wrote: " . . . the scenery, if I may use such an expression, appeared to the sight harmonious." However, this seeming paradise is disturbed by cyclones, for Mauritius is in the southern Indian Ocean cyclone belt. The cyclone season is December to April, and January to February is the peak period. Although most cyclones bypass the island, it lies in the path of some severe ones. The violent cyclones are long-remembered for the havoc they cause.

Cyclones form over the south-west Indian Ocean where the northerly and southerly trade winds meet. They are also known as tropical revolving storms, because the wind blows round an area in which the lowest pressure is at the centre. In simple terms, cyclones are very strong winds which can uproot even huge trees. They are accompanied by torrential rains, and the sea becomes very rough indeed.

In days gone by, people were less cyclone-conscious than they are today. They built flimsy buildings which were soon brought down by the violent winds. As a result many people lost their lives. Nowadays, houses are no longer built only of wood as

Looking towards the mountainous centre of the island. Charles Darwin wrote that the scenery seemed "harmonious"

they were in the old days. Most buildings are now made of concrete, although poor people use corrugated iron sheets to build their homes, and use boulders to hold down the roofs. The meterological office, too, is better equipped. During a cyclone the winds are recorded on instruments called anemometers. These measure the force and speed of the wind.

Before a cyclone arrives, the air becomes very still. Temperature and humidity are high. As the front of the cyclone arrives, the wind blows at about 160 kilometres (100 miles) per hour. The sky is dark and the rain falls in torrents. When

11

conditions become calm again it means that the "eye of the cyclone" has arrived. The population is told not to go out although everything outside seems calm. However, very soon the heavy rain starts again and the violent winds blow from the opposite direction to that of the front of the cyclone.

When a cyclone is known to be coming towards Mauritius, the radio and television stations warn the population of it. Cyclone Warning Class One means that a cyclone is in the area; Cyclone Warning Class Two is the alert-signal to prepare to take shelter; Cyclone Warning Class Three is issued when a cyclone appears imminent. It means that everyone should go indoors and take all the necessary precautions, such as closing windows, and bringing down television antennae. Cyclone Warning Class Four indicates that gusts of wind have exceeded 130 kilometres (80 miles) an hour over the whole or part of the island, and that it is dangerous to go out of doors. Those whose homes are not solid enough to protect them usually go to a cyclone shelter near where they live. The names of these shelters are announced regularly on the radio.

Often, during a cyclone, among the first things to be damaged are electricity wires and poles. So people have to be prepared and to have alternative ways of cooking their food and lighting their homes for a few days at least. The telephone is also very soon out of action. After a bad cyclone, "the island looks like a plucked chicken", in the words of a former governor, Sir Hubert Jerningham. Trees become uprooted, boats sink, the homes of the poorer people are destroyed.

A list of cyclones which have affected Mauritius has been produced by the metereological office. The severe cyclone which occurred on 2 May, 1703, left the plantations devastated and many houses destroyed. It is reported that, when the water receded in one part of the island a large number of drowned stags were found in the tree tops, suspended by their horns. The cyclone which hit the island on 21 January, 1748, was particularly violent. Bridges were carried away, a hospital was blown down and the Governor's Residence at Mon Plaisir was unroofed.

It is not only tin shanties and wooden houses which do not weather cyclones. During the violent cyclone of 28 February, 1818, large houses, some of which were built mainly of stone, were also blown down. Out of sixty ships in the harbour only four were left upright and even these were damaged.

One of the worst cyclones occurred in the last century, on 29 April, 1892, when gusts of wind may have exceeded 240 kilometres (150 miles) per hour. Until Cyclone Carol occurred on 28 February, 1960, the 1892 cyclone was said to have been the worst recorded. It left much devastation and human misery behind it. During Cyclone Carol, the highest gust of wind recorded was 278 kilometres (173 miles) per hour. Cyclones are traditionally given women's names. Sometimes people call their daughters after a cyclone.

Even if a cyclone does not hit Mauritius, when one is near by it can still cause damage. At the same time, however, the rains which accompany cyclones can be very beneficial to

13

agriculture, especially to the sugar-cane which is the life-line of the island's population.

After a cyclone there is a feeling of relief coupled with despair. Damage has to be repaired, trees planted again, gardens put in order. However, Mauritians have learned to live with cyclones and, after taking all the precautions they can, simply keep their fingers crossed when a cyclone approaches.

Mauritius has hills and mountains. The highest mountain is Piton de la Rivière Noire which is 827 metres (2,713 feet) high. Pieter Both mountain named after an early Dutch Governor, is slightly lower but much more impressive. It is a difficult mountain to climb and several people have lost their lives in the attempt. One party who got to the top in 1864 left a visitors' book in a tin so that others who succeeded could sign it!

Although the original dense forest no longer exists, there are still extensive patches of it preserved. Forest lands are now controlled by the Forests Department which has a programme for creating new forests. The Macchabee Forest, for example, is an interesting place in which to observe nature. There are also several waterfalls on the island, as well as twelve major rivers. The longest river is the Grand River South East which is 39 kilometres (24 miles) long.

In all parts of the island, women and girls can be seen on the river banks. Many of the poor people do not have running water in their homes so they wash their clothes in the river, scrubbing them on the stones. They leave them to dry on the

One of the impressive waterfalls of Mauritius, surrounded by forest

grass or on bushes and collect them later in the day. Mauritius also has lakes and reservoirs which keep the island supplied with water.

The Dutch, who first colonized Mauritius, destroyed many of the ebony forests. The ebony of Mauritius was said to be as black as tar and as polished as ivory. Later on, the French and the English cut down most of the other original forest trees in order to plant sugar and vegetables. However, there are still many interesting and beautiful trees in Mauritius. Some are indigenous (native) trees. Others have been brought from abroad. It has been said that the island itself is really like a huge tropical garden. One of the most curious trees is the Talipot palm which may live as long as seventy-five years before flowering just once, and then dying. Another unusual tree is the Ravenala or traveller's tree. It is shaped like an enormous fan, and its leaves have hollow bases from which, it has been reported, travellers can obtain drinkable water.

An abundance of bougainvillea grows in lovely colours all over the island. Orchids too, are cultivated. They are exported, as are the anthuriums and andreanums. Unfortunately many species of rare and local plants which grow wild are slowly being destroyed by people who collect firewood on which to cook. They do not seem to realize that at the same time they are destroying rare flowers, plants and ferns.

A great deal of fruit grows in Mauritius during the summer months. Pineapples grow all the year round but avocado pears, lychees and mangoes have a short season and are only available during the hot months. Some of the other fruits which grow in Mauritius are guavas, longanes, jujubes, pawpaws and jamalacs, as well as the coeur de boeuf and its cousin the atte. A Mauritian delicacy is the palm heart; this has been eaten since the Dutch lived on the island.

Since the island was originally unihabited for so many millions of years, the birds and reptiles had lived unmolested. With the coming of man, many of these became extinct. The destruction of the Mauritian forests had a further adverse effect on island fauna. However, Gerald Durrell, the Director of the Jersey Wildlife Preservation Trust, is doing what he can to help the Mauritian Government to save as much of its unique fauna as possible. Rare species, such as the pink pigeon, the Mauritian Kestrel and Merle, and the Mauritian Falcon (said to be one of the rarest birds in the world), are being bred in Jersey, in captivity. But Gerald Durrell believes that such rare animals should be bred in their own country. So he has set up a scholarship scheme to allow young people to train abroad and then come back home to breed rare creatures in captivity in their own countries. Mauritians were the first to benefit from this scheme.

From Earliest Times to French Occupation

It is probable that the early Phoenicians and the Malayo-Polynesians visited the Mascarene Islands on their journeys. From about the seventh century AD, Arab sailors were trading with the East African coast and with Madagascar. They sailed in strong vessels called dhows. An old Arab chart shows Mauritius as *Dinarobin*, meaning "island of silver". Arab pirates are said to have buried their treasure on all three Mascarene Islands.

The Portuguese pilot Diego Fernandez Pereira recorded the sighting of the island on 20 February, 1507. He named it Cirne after his ship. In the sixteenth century, Mauritius could have been regarded as paradise. It was free from disease, its birds were beautiful, and its forests were full of ebony and other trees. Its streams were full of pure, fresh water. There were water buffaloes and wild bulls on the island but there were no dangerous animals.

In 1598, Mauritius became a Dutch possession. The early Dutch visitors to Mauritius provided the oldest available description of the island. It was named at that time in honour of Count Maurice of Nassau, then *stadthouder* (ruler) of Holland.

The Dutch found enormous tortoises (now extinct) on the backs of which six men could stand at the same time. They

An unspoilt area of Mauritius, reminiscent of the "paradise" found by the first Portuguese and Dutch visitors

caught dodos and ate sea-cows. The dodo was an easy prey—not only to man but also to monkeys, rats and wild pigs, as it was a bird which could not fly. Within a century, it became extinct. (The expression "as dead as a dodo" is still used today.) But, in 1865, Lewis Carroll made the dodo famous when his book *Alice's Adventures in Wonderland* was first published. In that same year George Clark, an English schoolmaster then living in Mauritius, dug up bones belonging to a dodo.

Another large flightless bird to be found in Mauritius (and nowhere else in the world) had the curious name of Aphanapteryx. This, too, has been extinct since the seventeenth

19

The dodo, a flightless bird which is now extinct

century. Paintings executed by travellers who had seen the bird show that it had a long curved beak and rust-red feathers, but had no wings at all.

In the seventeenth century, vessels stopped at Mauritius to stock up with food and water. The sailors also cut down trees to obtain timber with which to repair their ships. Then they took away all the ebony they could carry, and sold it for a great deal of money in Europe.

Mauritius was not considered important by the Dutch. In 1652, they had founded the Cape Colony in South Africa. The Dutch were already well-established in Batavia, a city they built on the site of the old town of Djakarta in Java. In fact, the first cuttings of sugar-cane, and the first stags, were introduced to Mauritius from Java by the Dutch. Unknowingly the Dutch thus laid the foundations of the sugar-based economy of Mauritius. Stag-hunting continues to give Mauritians pleasure to this day. The Dutch also left on the island useful plants, fruit trees and livestock, especially cattle. Mauritius also became full of rats which had swum to land from the ships which called there. As the years went by, the rats became more and more numerous.

From 1656 to 1658 many employees of the Dutch East India Company were sent to the settlements in the Cape and Batavia. The Dutch in Mauritius depended on slaves and some convicts from Batavia for their manual labour. But many of these escaped and hid in the dense forests. They soon became a source of danger and terror, as they came back to kill their former masters.

When the first Dutch settlers left Mauritius in 1658, they destroyed everything that could have been useful to their English and French enemies—the plantations, the buildings and the fort.

From 1664 to 1710 the Dutch East India Company made a second attempt to settle on Mauritius, but they failed again. The cyclones and the rats discouraged them. Their slaves also kept on escaping into the forest, so that there were not enough people to help the Dutch develop the colony. Both the first two Governors died on the island. In 1706, there was a drought. And, in 1707, the Company decided to leave Mauritius. In 1710, after eighty-two years of occupation, the last of the Dutch finally departed, having cut down many of the ebony forests. Again,

21

Mauritius became a haven for pirates who landed when they needed fresh water, food and shelter.

The pirates had founded a small republic on Ile Sainte Marie on the east coast of Madagascar. This republic was called Libertalia. One of its founders was a defrocked monk, named Carracioli, who had lost a leg. Amongst the most famous pirates were John Bowen, Nathaniel North, Captain Taylor (who had a wooden leg), Olivier Levasseur (known as La Buse), Malroux, Le Vaillant, Trehouart and Dutertre. However, those who know about pirates say that Ripaud de Montaudevert was more audacious and daring than any of the others.

Ships in the Indian Ocean had to contend not only with pirates but with corsairs (privateers) as well. The pirate was a thief who looted ships of all nations, including his own. He was considered an outlaw, and was hanged on the spot if captured. But the corsair was different. He was a "gentleman thief". He was given a "letter of marque" by his own government. This gave him permission to raid ships belonging to his country's enemies. The corsair never attacked vessels belonging to his own country or its friends. The pirates and corsairs attacked many French ships going to Pondichery in French India. This was one of the reasons which encouraged France to occupy Mauritius.

On 20 September, 1715, a French captain named Guillaume Dufresne d'Arsel landed on the island and took possession of it in the name of the King of France. He renamed it Ile de France. From nearby Bourbon (now called Réunion) a few families and soldiers are said to have gone to colonize Ile de

A river scene in Mauritius today. This river may have provided drinking water for pirates when they put in here long ago

France. But they found life there too primitive. They firmly planted the French flag to show that the island was French, and then they left.

The French government granted a concession over Ile de France to the French East India Company. The Company ran the island from 1721 to 1767. The French colonists found it hard to work in the fields. So they took slaves from Madagascar, Mozambique and West Africa to work for them. Most slaves were expected to work from sunrise to sunset every day except Sundays. From 1723, the *Code Noir* had to be followed in French colonies. These were laws concerning slavery. One of the laws was that all slaves should be baptized as Roman Catholics. If they were not, their masters had to pay a fine.

The first Governor of the French East India Company, in 1722, was Denis de Nyon. He was followed in 1725 by Denis de Brousse and, in 1727, by Pierre Benoît who was also called Dumas. Nicolas de Maupin governed from 1729 to 1735. In between there were other Governors for short periods. In 1735, Bertrand François Mahé de Labourdonnais was sent out by the Company as Governor General of the Mascarenes. He was a man of many talents and was to become the most famous Governor of them all. "Labourdonnais," one historian writes, "made three significant contributions to the history of Mauritius: the creation of a well-equipped port, the provision of a regular supply of food and the establishment of internal order." Among other things, he opened the first sugar factory, and was responsible for the exploration of the Seychelles whose destiny was, for years to come, to be linked to that of Mauritius.

On the 17/18 August, 1744, the sailing-ship *St Geran* sank off the coast of Ile de France. In the eighteenth century this was a tragic but, alas, common event. However, this particular tragedy was to make the island known all over the world, because some years later, Jacques Henri Bernardin de St Pierre (who came to Mauritius as a Royal Engineer) stayed on the island from 1768 to 1770 and learned about the shipwreck. Bernardin de St Pierre was also a philosopher and novelist and he wrote a novel based on this incident. This novel, which became famous, is called *Paul et Virginie*—the names of the hero and

24

heroine. These two young people, who loved each other, both die at the end of the book. Virginie drowned in the *St Geran* (in the story) and Paul died of a broken heart.

The *St Geran* had on board 54,000 Spanish *piastres* destined for Bourbon (now Réunion). It was also carrying the machinery for the first sugar factory which was then being constructed on Ile de France. In 1966, an underwater diver discovered the wreck of the *St Geran* while looking for fish. The wreck is now in the naval museum of the town of Mahébourg.

A statue of Paul and Virginie, the hero and heroine of a novel by Bernardin de St. Pierre

After the departure of Labourdonnais in 1746, Ile de France was ruled by four Governors General. They were Pierre Félix Barthélémy David, René Magon, Jean Baptiste Charles Bouvet de Lozier and Antoine Marie Desforges-Boucher. All four Governors encouraged agriculture but their efforts did not seem to meet with much success. According to a report dated 1765, the inhabitants were not interested in farming. All they wanted was to make their fortune as fast as they could and then take their money back to France.

During this period, British ships were being captured by corsairs, many of whom lived in Mauritius. However, the Anglo-French Wars of 1756-63 kept the British busy. These wars ruined the French East India Company. It could no longer maintain its concessions in the Indian Ocean. Ile de France was one of these concessions. So, in 1767, the French government took over the administration of the island which, by now, had a population of 18,800.

The royal decree which placed Mauritius under the control of the French Crown took effect on 14 July, 1767. On that day a Governor General and an Intendant landed at the capital, Port Louis. The Governor General, Daniel Dumas, held surpreme power and was commander of the islands' naval and military forces. The Intendant (or administrator) was Pierre Poivre and he was responsible mainly for the financial administration of the island. Dumas and Poivre quarrelled a great deal and, after being Governor for only sixteen months, Dumas had to be recalled to France. He was succeeded by

François Julien du Dresnay, Chevalier Desroches. Although Poivre had many disagreements with him too, these two administrators managed to accomplish some useful work. They improved Port Louis, and its harbour, which was full of the wreckage of ships destroyed by cyclones. They reorganized the shipyards and built roads which linked the outlying districts to the capital. Poivre also tried to establish plantations of cloves and nutmeg, as he knew Ile de France could get good prices for such spices in Europe. However, his attempt failed.

Desroches was succeeded by Charles Louis d'Arzac, Chevalier de Ternay (1772-76), Antoine de Guiran, Chevalier de La Brillane (1776-79), Viscomte François de Souillac (1779-87) and Antoine Joseph Raimond de Bruni, Chevalier d'Entrescasteaux (1787-89). They were all naval officers and they managed to create some order through their firm and disciplined government.

It was in January 1790 that news of the French Revolution was first brought to Port Louis. The Governor General at this time was the Comte de Conway, who was of Irish origin. The inhabitants of Ile de France imitated the revolutionary activity in France by forming Jacobite Clubs with such names as *Sans-Culottes* and *Chevaliers d'Industrie*. They even erected a guillotine. Fortunately, only a sheep was beheaded. Just one act of bloodshed was committed—when some soldiers murdered Count Macnamara, commandant of the French Navy in the Indian Ocean.

On 4 February, 1794, France decreed that slavery should be

27

abolished in all its colonies, and that slave-owners should not get any money or compensation for the slaves whom they had bought but now had to set free. The inhabitants of Mauritius did not agree to this. They were aware that in Haiti the slaves had revolted, killed most members of the European community there and destroyed what had taken years to build.

The inhabitants of Ile de France decided not to obey the mother-country. They did not free their slaves. The Colonial Assemblies governing the island prohibited the further importation of slaves. But they continued to be smuggled in all the same.

In 1796, two agents were sent from France to persuade Ile de France to obey orders, but they were soon forced to leave. France was busy fighting England at the time and could do little to punish the faraway rebels. Perhaps it turned a blind eye because it did not want to see more bloodshed like that in Haiti. In Ile de France there were, in any case, about eight slaves to every free man. If the slaves had decided to organize themselves they could have easily revolted and taken over the colony. For various reasons, they did not.

A great deal of damage was being inflicted at this time on ships of the British East India Company, particularly by French corsairs. This privateering (so-called because it was a kind of private warfare) against the enemy, was so profitable that sometimes merchant seamen abandoned their ships and took on the more exciting career of corsair. It was a profitable career, too, since the Indian Ocean was one of the world's most

A figure of the Virgin Mary. The Catholic religion was first introduced into Mauritius by the French colonists

important commercial routes and the ships which passed that way were full of expensive cargo. The most famous corsair of all was Robert Surcouf who was justly called "the king of corsairs". The English were afraid even of his name as he did

29

Cutting sugar-cane. When the island was called Ile de France, the plantations were worked by imported slaves

them a great deal of harm, and they never managed to capture him. Like his brother Nicholas, also a corsair, Robert was made Chevalier de la Légion d'Honneur, the highest honour France can award. The eldest Surcouf brother, Charles (also a corsair in his time), is said to be buried in Mauritius.

At the end of the eighteenth century, Britain held all the key positions in the Indian Ocean. At the time there was a great deal of rivalry between the English and the French in India. However, what Pitt, then prime minister of England, had said in 1761 remained true: "As long as the French hold Ile de France, the British will never be masters of India." Ile de France was close to both India and Madagascar and, because it was so isolated, French ships could gather there without their enemies' knowledge.

On December 15, 1803, Ile de France was visited by a distinguished Englishman called Mathew Flinders (1774-1814). Flinders, a cartographer and navigator, arrived from Australia. As a boy, he had read Daniel Defoe's *Robinson Crusoe*. This so fired his imagination that he came to love travel and adventure, and he decided to go to sea.

When Flinders landed in Mauritius the French Governor was Charles Mathieu Isidore, Comte Decaen. England and France were at war again. Decaen thought Flinders was a spy and had him locked up with other prisoners of war. However, after some time he was transferred to an estate, and he lived with a Mauritian family for five years. During this time he worked on a history of his voyages. After being released in 1810, he returned to England, where he spent three years writing his famous book *Voyage to Terra Australis*. Flinders died at the age of forty on the very day his book was published—July 14, 1814. His book gives an interesting account of the Mauritians of his day.

On 23 August, 1810, a British fleet of four ships engaged a French squadron (also of four ships) near Ile de la Passe, east of Mahébourg, and a famous naval battle lasting four days was fought. This Battle of Grand Port, as it is called, was won by the French. It was the only French naval victory in the Napoleonic Wars. Remains of the sunken English ships were recovered a century later and can now be seen in the naval history museum in Mahébourg.

A few months later, the British gathered together many more men and arms on the island of Rodrigues—560 kilometres (350 miles) to the east of Mauritius. From there, some ten thousand men landed on Mauritius near Cap Malheureux and at once began to march towards Port Louis. The French Governor, Comte Decaen, realized that he did not have enough soldiers to fight the British. He also wanted to avoid unnecessary bloodshed. He had asked France for more soldiers and money but his request had been ignored. And so, on 3 December, 1810, the French surrendered, after ninety years of occupation. The Indian Ocean became "a British lake", and Ile de France was called Mauritius once again.

From British Colonization to Independence

Since the time of the Dutch, Mauritius had always had a military governor. However, Sir Robert Farquhar, the first British Governor of Mauritius, was a civilian. He invited the French subjects of Mauritius to swear loyalty to King George III of England. The registers in which they signed are preserved in the archives in Mauritius.

Several disasters were to befall Mauritius in the years which followed. In September 1816, a great fire broke out in the commercial quarter of Port Louis and destroyed vast quantities of stock and much property. In 1818 and 1819 cyclones ruined the crops. To prevent famine, shiploads of corn were brought from nearby Bourbon and then from India.

Port Louis is surrounded by a chain of mountains which makes it very hot, especially in summer. Diseases brought to Mauritius from other parts of the world used to spread easily, especially as standards of cleanliness were low and the inhabitants were not strong enough to resist infection. In 1811, a smallpox epidemic broke out, but this was quickly controlled by vaccination. In 1813, rabies struck the island and 2,300 dogs were killed in two days. However, the cholera epidemic of 1819 was not so easily controlled, and fifteen thousand people died from it.

33

A general view of Port Louis, the capital of Mauritius, which was largely rebuilt after the destruction caused by fire in 1816

Farquhar noticed that when cyclones hit the island, sugar was far less damaged than any other crop. So he advised planters to grow more sugar. At this time the government also built roads so that people could travel in horsedrawn coaches. Until about 1828, men travelled on horseback or on donkeys and women travelled in palanquins. It sometimes required many slaves to transport these covered portable couches from one part on the island to another.

Under Sir Lowry Cole, who was Governor from 1823 to 1828, sugar became extremely important. Duties on sugar exported to Britain had been higher that those paid by other colonies.

A modern sugar-cane plantation. Under the governorship of Sir Lowry Cole (1823 to 1828) sugar became extremely important in Mauritius

Under Cole, these sugar duties were reduced and people were therefore encouraged to plant sugar. In 1810, there were about 4,050 hectares (10,000 acres) of sugar-cane. Twenty years later, in 1830, there were 20,235 hectares (50,000 acres). Eighty-five per cent of the colony's income came from sugar export to Britain. The planters needed more slaves to work in the plantations but, due to the 1813 law forbidding new slaves to enter Mauritius, these had to be brought secretly.

By now the Anti-slavery Society in Britain was determined to end slavery in British colonies. In 1828, through the efforts of Dr Stephen Lushington (one of its members), a law was passed in the British Parliament which officially abolished the colour bar—discrimination—not only in Mauritius, but in all British colonies. Until this law was passed, black and Indian boys were not allowed to enter the most important government school in Mauritius, Royal College. It was reserved for white boys only. There were many other acts of discrimination, but these were now slowly becoming less frequent.

Unlike the case in other British colonies, such as the West Indies, most of the planters in Mauritius were French—and France had been an enemy of England for a long time. So French planters had no friends in the British Parliament to defend their interests. The Anti-slavery Society knew this and tried to

Dr. Stephen Lushington, an influential member of the Anti-Slavery Society

A poster advertising the Mauritius Commercial Bank founded in 1838

persuade the British Parliament to abolish slavery without paying the French slave-owners any compensation. They hoped that once this policy was accepted in Mauritius it would be accepted in other colonies too. The planters in Mauritius realized this. They therefore chose Adrien d'Epinay, a young lawyer, to speak on their behalf. D'Epinay went twice to Britain and finally persuaded the Secretary of State in London to pay slave-owners an indemnity (money as compensation). The Secretary of State also agreed to allow Mauritius to have a Council of Government which would include some of the island's inhabitants. This council would advise the British Governor on how to govern the island.

Adrien d'Epinay returned to Mauritius in 1831. In 1832 he started a newspaper called *Le Cernéen*. Until then, the chief newspaper had been the *Government Gazette* which was heavily

37

censored. *Le Cernéen* became a leading free newspaper and it continued in print for many years. It closed its doors in 1982.

The Anti-Slavery Society in Britain was still not happy that slave-owners were going to be paid indemnity. To make this payment in all the colonies was going to cost the British government millions of pounds. By sending one of their members to Mauritius, they hoped to persuade Mauritians to free their slaves without compensation.

The man they sent was John Jeremie who had written a collection of essays about slavery in which he stated his views very clearly. He thought it more important for slaves to be given their freedom than for sugar colonies to be saved. Jeremie was unpopular in "that rebellious island" even before he set foot in it. When he arrived, in 1832, the shops were closed, and government employees and even judges did not go to work in protest. After all, most of them owned slaves and they did not like Jeremie's views! He returned to Britain after seven weeks but went back to Mauritius again, in April 1833, and for another eighteen months.

In 1835, the slaves were officially freed. However, they were to remain with their masters as apprentices. This was partly so that they could learn some useful trade to prepare them for independence, but also because the planters wanted to make sure that there would be other workers to replace them. Indemnity was paid in 1835 for 56,600 slaves. Altogether, Mauritian slave-owners received two million pounds. In 1838, Mauritian and English merchants started the Mauritius

38

Indian women on Tamarin beach. Many Mauritians are of Indian origin, descended from immigrants who first came to the island in 1834

Commercial Bank. Most of the money invested in it came from the compensation received for slaves. This bank has become an important Mauritian institution.

Since 1834, even before slavery was officially abolished, Indian immigrants had been introduced into the island in larger numbers that ever before. They were soon to play an important role in the sugar industry for, by 1839, most apprentices had left their masters. They could no longer bear the idea of working on the plantations which reminded them that they had once been slaves. Some became fishermen, others independent peasants. Many went to Port Louis where they found work. Only four thousand ex-slaves signed one-year contracts to continue working on the plantations.

The history of Mauritius under the British mainly concerns the sugar industry. Most of the thousands of Indians brought to the island were made to work in the sugar plantations or in jobs connected with the industry in one way or another, such as the building of roads and reservoirs. Fewer alternative crops were grown and some forests were destroyed in order to make way for more sugar. As Mauritius was now part of the British Empire it had a huge market for its sugar. The island was becoming a single-crop economy.

In 1847, ten years after Queen Victoria became Queen of England, Mauritius issued its first stamps. There is an interesting story connected with these two events. The use of French in the Mauritian law courts was forbidden by the British

A reminder of British colonial times — a statue of Queen Victoria in Port Louis

as from 15 July, 1847. Much bitterness was provoked by this decision as most of the members of the legal profession at the time were French-speaking. Sir William Gomm, the British Governor, became very unpopular. And so, in order to help restore good relations between the British and the French, Lady Gomm organized a ball. The invitations were despatched by post on 21 September, 1847, and the envelopes were stamped with first-ever postage stamps issued by a British colony.

A set of stamps comprising the one penny and twopenny denominations was put on sale. The engraving of the printing plates was entrusted to a watchmaker and jeweller by the name of Joseph Barnard. It soon became obvious that an error had been made. In the wording on the stamps, ''Post Office'' instead of ''Post Paid'' had been printed. This error has made these penny stamps amongst the rarest in the world. Fourteen copies of the penny stamps and twelve of the twopenny stamp are believed to be still in existence and would now sell for a very high price.

Between 1840 and 1870, there were epidemics of cholera and malaria on the island. In three years, malaria killed about seventy thousand people out of a population of three hundred and fifty thousand. It was not realized then that the disease is spread by the bite of certain mosquitoes. Further troubles were to come. In 1868 Mauritius was hit by a violent cyclone. The next year, the island lost most of its importance as a port of call and a good deal of its foreign income when the Suez Canal

A signpost in Mauritius today. In spite of agreeing that the island should retain its own languages, the British introduced English

was opened. Ships could now sail straight from the Mediterranean to the Indian Ocean without having to sail all round Africa. They therefore no longer needed to stop at Port Louis harbour. However, the opening of the Suez Canal did bring some advantages to Mauritius in that it allowed the islanders to have better and faster communications with Europe.

Under the terms of the capitulation (surrender) signed in 1810, under Decaen, the British had agreed that the inhabitants of the island should keep their religion, language, laws and customs. Between 1840 and 1870, however, the British

42

A country road with a modern surface. The most significant improvements in Mauritius' roads took place under British rule

government tried to anglicize Mauritius. They started by organizing Royal College, the most important government school on the island, in the style of an English school with an English rector. Until then it had been like a French *lycée*.

After Sir William Gomm took the unpopular decision of making English compulsory in the law courts (instead of French), further changes took place. Anglican clergymen were brought out to help build Anglican churches and schools. English, rather than French, was used whenever possible.

During this period still better roads were built; and, in 1864, a railway was begun.

43

This family are the descendants of Indians who arrived in Mauritius during the nineteenth century

Jaodish Mohur

Indian immigrants continued to arrive in Mauritius until 1909. They lived in small huts on sugar estates; and they had very few possessions. In fact, it is said that they were more comfortable in prison than in their homes because at least there they did not have to work! Between 1871 and 1873 Sir Arthur Hamilton Gordon was Governor of Mauritius. He was outspoken about the way in which the Indians were being treated. But this made him very unpopular with the planters. In 1872, however, a Royal Commission was set up to look into the treatment of Indians. Two English lawyers, William Edward

44

Frere and Victor Alexander Williamson went to Mauritius to hold an enquiry. The planters received a great deal of criticism in the final report. As a result, in 1878, a new Labour Law was passed which improved the position of the Indian immigrants.

As well as providing help for the Indians, the British tried to be fair to the Mauritian people as a whole. Sir John Pope-Hennessy, an Irishman who served as Governor between 1883 and 1889, believed that Mauritians should be allowed to govern themselves. In 1886, thanks to the intervention of Pope-Hennessy, Mauritius had its first elected Legislative Council. From then onwards the Council of Government consisted of a mixture of members: nine officials, nine members nominated by the Governor and, most important of all, ten members elected by male Mauritians.

Those who voted had to have an income of at least fifty rupees per month, or had to own or rent property which was considered to be "substantial". Almost all who were allowed to vote exercised their votes. The first Indian member of Council was nominated in 1886. This was a very important achievement for the Indian immigrant community and for Mauritian democracy.

Because Pope-Hennessy did not always sympathize with the planters, they too tried to get rid of him. Some even said he was mad. As a result, the British government decided to recall him to Britain. However, the Mauritians sent Sir William Newton, a Mauritian lawyer, to defend Sir John and he convinced the British government to send the Governor back to continue serving in Mauritius. A statue was erected in his

45

honour in Port Louis. Another statue was erected near by, in honour of his friend, Sir William Newton.

Towards the end of the nineteenth century, Mauritius was once more the victim of epidemics and cyclones. The smallpox epidemic of 1891-2 caused over one thousand deaths. The cyclone of 1892 was the origin of much damage and misery. In two hours hundreds of people were made homeless, sugar estates were badly damaged and many merchants lost their property. As if this were not enough, in 1893 a fire broke out in Port Louis creating even more devastation.

Six years later, the island was struck by bubonic plague, caused by rats. This killed more than one thousand inhabitants, mostly in Port Louis. At last, the Mauritians began to realize the importance of hygiene and of vaccination to protect them from disease.

Port Louis declined in the nineteenth century (although it was to regain some of its importance at a later stage in its history). In addition, as a result of the various catastrophes which had struck there, many inhabitants of Port Louis left to start a new life in the town of Curepipe. Because of its position—on a plateau—Curepipe has much more rain and a cooler climate than Port Louis. By 1900, Curepipe was beginning to be regarded as the capital of Mauritius.

Other people who had previously lived in Port Louis began building new homes in Vacoas, Rose Hill, Beau Bassin and Quatre-Bornes. These towns slowly became important residential areas.

46

A plantation house. Some planters became very rich in the 1920s

By the beginning of the twentieth century, over-population was already beginning to be a problem in Mauritius. Sugar prices were not going up and, as a result of this and of over-population, many Mauritians emigrated. Then came the First World War (1914-18) and, once again, the British paid a very good price for Mauritian sugar. As the island was a British colony at this time, many of the islanders went to Europe to fight in the British and French armies, against Germany. A large number of these soldiers died in the war, but some of them had distinguished military careers—one Mauritian, named Henri Coutanceau, became a general in the French army.

In 1920, England was paying five times the usual price for Mauritian sugar. As a result, the island became very prosperous. Some planters became extremely rich and the plantation workers

47

A colonial house near Beau Bassin, built in the 1830s

were earning a great deal of money. The Governor of the time wisely used some of the money earned to improve schools, houses and other services.

Indeed, throughout the beginning of the twentieth century many improvements were carried out. The first aeroplane was introduced, and a radio service was started. Mauritians became less isolated. By now, the major towns had electricity and more and more telephones were being installed. Cars and buses were also introduced.

By 1927, the sugar industry was again having problems. Britain had many difficulties itself and could not do much to help Mauritius. Islanders were encouraged to grow aloes, tobacco, pineapples and other products, as it was considered that Mauritius depended too much on one crop. Since a great

48

A view of Government House, built during the colonial period

many sacks were needed for the transport of sugar, a factory was opened where sacks could be made locally from aloe fibre.

Under the governorship of Sir Wilfred Jackson, the sugar industry recovered. The government lent planters money at a very low rate of interest. Then, in 1937, in spite of low sugar prices, the labourers felt that they should be earning higher wages. For the first time in the history of the Mauritian sugar industry, serious riots broke out, and several labourers were killed. An enquiry was held and, as a result, the labourers were given higher wages.

Sir Bede Clifford, who was the Governor of Mauritius between 1937 and 1942, planned to make many changes which would improve the lot of the workers and the economy of Mauritius. However, these had to be abandoned when the

A pineapple ripening. The cultivation of fruit has been encouraged to reduce the country's dependence on the sugar plantations

Second World War broke out in 1939. One positive effect of the war was that, in 1940, the island regained the importance it had enjoyed before the opening of the Suez Canal. Because Italy had sided with Germany to fight Great Britain and its allies, it was no longer safe for ships to pass through the Mediterranean Sea. They began to pass round the Cape of Good Hope, stopping at Mauritius to take on food, water and other supplies.

More labour riots broke out in 1943. Because of the shortages caused by the war, the price of most goods had risen, although wages had not been increased. The people's diet also changed. Mauritians had been used to eating imported rice but as it was no longer possible to import this during the war, rice was replaced by maize, manioc and sweet potatoes which were grown on the sugar estates.

50

In 1948, Mauritius was given a new constitution in which there were fewer officials in the Legislative Council and more elected members. Mauritians of every class and race were to be represented. Although the constitutional and electoral reforms

An Indian worker picking tea in Mauritius today

of 1948 were very limited, the white sugar planters began to realize that political power would eventually go to the majority—which was, and continues to be, the descendants of the indentured Indian labourers.

To fight what the white planters called the "Indian Menace", they enlisted the help of political allies in other racial groups. The Creoles (of mixed African and white descent) for example, were afraid that as the Indians gained power, they (the Creoles) would lose it. Many Creoles worked as civil servants and they feared they would be replaced by educated Indians.

The descendants of the African slaves who had once worked in the plantations were poor people, many of whom were unemployed. They too joined the Whites, the Creoles, the Chinese and the Muslims who all feared that the far more numerous Indians would become too influential. Somewhat surprisingly, the descendants of the slaves were now allied with the descendants of the original planters who had been the slave-owners.

The Indians—under the banner of the Mauritius Labour Party—wanted Mauritius to become independent of Britain and to govern itself. The Whites, Creoles, Africans, Muslims and Chinese—under the banner of the Parti Mauricien Social Democrate—were in favour of integration or association with Britain. Eventually, many Indians who worked on the sugar estates also joined this party.

The leader of the PMSD wanted to hold a referendum, to let the people decide whether they wished their country to

Mauritian Indians—Indians enthusiastically supported the idea of an independent Mauritius when this was first proposed

become independent of Britain or to integrate with it. But the referendum was never held, for Britain was not interested in integration—it wanted Mauritius to become independent.

However, Britain was interested in the Indian Ocean which, by the 1960s, had again become very important because it lies between Europe and the sources of petroleum. After many discussions and an election which the Mauritius Labour Party won by a small majority, Mauritius was granted its independence in 1968. In exchange, Britain was to be given the island of Diego Garcia (part of the Chagos Archipelago) in the middle of the Indian Ocean.

As part of the independence deal, the two thousand or so

A parade celebrating the anniversary of Mauritian independence

The Mauritian flag—a symbol of the nation's independence

people who lived on Diego Garcia were gradually moved to Mauritius. Sixty per cent of them are of African and Malagasy origin and forty per cent of Indian, especially Tamil, origin. Every country has to pay a price for its independence. There was no bloodshed in this case but the people of Diego Garcia lost the home they loved to make way for the independence of Mauritius.

A Nation of Immigrants

The Mauritians live peacefully side by side, in spite of their differences of race, religion, colour and culture. They have problems, of course. Unemployment, partly the result of over-population, sometimes causes tension between the different communities. But most people try to solve their problems as peacefully as possible.

Although the Mauritian population is made up of several ethnic groups—and could be called a nation of immigrants—it would be wrong to visualize Mauritian society as consisting solely of isolated communities. The Muslim lives next to the Chinese, and the Hindu next to the Afro-Mauritian (or Mauritian of African descent).

The population arrived in successive waves over the past three hundred years. It started to grow steadily under French rule in the eighteenth century. In 1735, twenty years after the island was taken over by the French, the population barely reached a thousand. By 1775, with an increasing slave trade and a large number of settlers coming in, the number stood at nearly thirty thousand. By the turn of the century, black slaves accounted for eighty-five per cent of the total population which had passed the 75,000 mark.

The abolition of slavery by the British in 1835 was to have

A Chinese child buying fruit from a street trader. Mauritius is a multi-racial country with different ethnic groups living peacefully side by side

an important impact on the population of the island. By then there were 100,000 people living in Mauritius. However, when they were no longer allowed to bring in slaves, the sugar-cane planters turned to India as a source of cheap labour. In the thirty years following the abolition of slavery, over 200,000 Indian labourers came to Mauritius to work, and most of them chose to stay.

By the end of the nineteenth century, the population stood at 370,000. Fifty years later it had reached half a million. And

57

A family planning poster in a Mauritian street. The total population is now over one million and the island is clearly over-populated

in 1968—the year Mauritius became independent—there were more than 700,000 inhabitants. Today, the total population is over one million. This is how an originally unpopulated island has become over-populated in a short period of time.

The smallest ethnic group of all is the white community, which is largely of French descent, and makes up two per cent of the total population. Many Frenchmen came to Mauritius in the early 1700s. Some (aristocrats) escaped from France after the French Revolution in 1769; others came in a spirit of adventure, to build a better life for themselves in what was then the new

58

A Chinese street trader. The Chinese now form about three per cent of the population of Mauritius. They are the second smallest group

French colony of Ile de France. Some were tradesmen, others were soldiers or sailors. Most came to make or remake their fortunes. The Whites (or Franco-Mauritians as they are often called because of their French origin) are very strong economically. Many of the sugar estates and major businesses on the island are managed by them. Nowadays, very few Whites marry members of other communities. They tend to marry amongst themselves or to marry foreigners.

The Chinese form the second smallest group in Mauritius today. They make up just over three per cent of the population.

They started coming to the island in large numbers in 1860. An attempt had been made previously to bring them to Mauritius as indentured labourers to work in the sugar-cane fields, but this had failed. The hard-working Chinese now control most of the Mauritian retail trade. Some have become wealthy businessmen. Others have entered professions such as medicine and law. There was a time when there were only two Chinese women in Mauritius for every one thousand Chinese men. Since then, there has been some intermarriage with Creoles. Many Chinese have become Christians; others have remained Buddhists.

A Chinese Buddhist pagoda in Port Louis

The Creoles, who are people of mixed descent, form about twenty-eight per cent of the population. During early colonial times in Mauritius, there were usually more men than women among the immigrants. Because of this, there was a great deal of intermarriage. Often the Creoles seem white but among their ancestors may have been Indians, Africans, Malagasy, Chinese or perhaps a mixture of these. The Creole community is very complex and can be sub-divided according to ancestry, wealth, education and, above all, colour. A percentage of the Creoles are of pure African descent, although this is very difficult to prove. The term Afro-Mauitian has recently been introduced to describe these people.

How did the Africans and Malagasy come to Mauritius? The first slaves were introduced into Mauritius between 1639 and 1645 when the Dutch East India Company, who had taken possession of the island, imported men and women from Madagascar as cheap labourers. In 1645, the Dutch signed a treaty with the king of the region of Antongil in the north of Madagascar. The king committed himself to furnish slaves only to Mauritius, and to no other colony.

However, many of the slaves escaped into the interior of the island. When additional slaves were brought in, many of them, too, joined the fugitive slaves, or maroons as they came to be called. The maroons preferred to live as outlaws than to have more comfortable surroundings without their freedom. They hunted in the forests and ate what they could find. Sometimes the maroons raided and burned the farms and houses of their old masters, often murdering them and setting other slaves at liberty. Is some parts of Mauritius it was actually unsafe for planters to travel without an escort of soldiers.

Some of the slaves had been captured in East Africa and brought to Mauritius against their will. In all, about forty-five per cent of them came from Mozambique, about forty per cent from Madagascar, about thirteen per cent from India and two per cent from West Africa. Sometimes they fought among themselves, for those who came from Madagascar hated the slaves who had been brought from East Africa.

All these slaves were, of course, brought to Mauritius by ship and, if they got the chance, they organized a revolt on board. This is known from the ships' records which have survived. In 1780, a slave named Bororo who admitted his part in such a revolt was shot and his body was thrown overboard. In another revolt, in 1803, four slaves threw themselves into the sea to escape slavery.

What was a typical day on board a slave-trader? About half an hour after sunrise, the slaves were brought up to the deck, four by four, to wash their faces and their hands in salt water, and to rinse out their mouths with vinegar to avoid scurvy (a disease which often attacked sailors due to too much salt and a lack of vegetables in their diet). The slaves then ate their first meal of the day. This usually consisted of rice and salted beef. During the whole crossing, which lasted about a month, they were given the same food, day in and day out.

After this, there was a long day ahead. Sometimes they

Sugar-cane cutters today—some are the descendants of slaves

worked making ropes. At four o'clock in the afternoon they ate more rice and salted beef. Then, if the weather was fine, they were allowed to sing and dance on deck. Once the sun went down, they returned to the hold of the ship. However, before being taken down, they were searched very carefully in case they had taken some object from the deck with which they could cut their chains. In any event, the crew always kept their guns at hand. The slaves then lay in rows in the hold of the ship, very close to each other. This was done so that as many slaves as possible could be brought in at the lowest cost.

In spite of the precautions taken, epidemics sometimes broke out on board the slave ships. Apart from scurvy, there was the dreaded disease of smallpox. The slaves were generally young, between eighteen and twenty-five, yet in 1739, out of 620 slaves bought in Mozambique, 360 perished during the voyage to Mauritius. In 1740, of eighty who embarked in Pondichery, in French India, only six arrived. And in 1777 on the ship *l'Aimable Victoire*, which was going from Mozambique to Port Louis, 119 out of the 422 slaves who embarked, died.

The idea of slavery shocks people today. But it was, at the time, universally accepted by the civilized world. It was considered impossible to run colonies without slaves. And, unfortunately, it was believed that slaves had to be kept under control since they greatly outnumbered their masters. So they were flogged for misbehaviour. It was considered that without

A plan showing how slaves were forced to lie in rows in the holds of the slave-trading ships which brought them to Mauritius

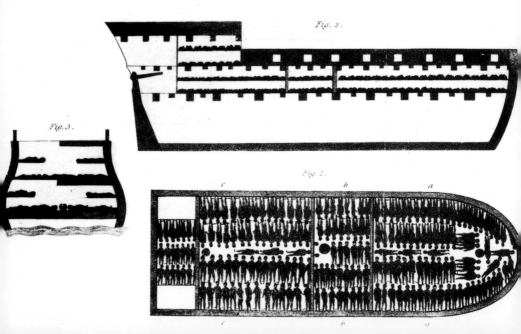

strict discipline and punishment there would be chaos on the plantations. At least, this was the philosophy of those who were trying to make a life in Ile de France.

Slave-trading was very common in many parts of the world in those days. It was not only the white man who indulged in it. The Arabs, for example, were great slave-traders; many of the slaves who were brought to Mauritius were sold by Arabs in Zanzibar, an island off the east coast of Africa. Indeed, by the 1850s, after the abolition of slavery, ''men-stealing and men-selling'' was being carried out by the Africans themselves. Many gave up trading in ivory and other traditional commodities simply because they earned much more money from trading in people. Many tribes became engaged in hunting and kidnapping their neighbours to sell as slaves to French ships. These slaves, however, were not destined for Mauritius.

Slavery was a cruel system and many tales are told of slaves who tried to return home by crossing the vast ocean which separated them from their native land. They did not believe their masters' advice that they could not possibly reach home in a small boat. The majority perished but there were some who succeeded. They persisted in undertaking this dangerous journey, in the belief that, even if they died, their spirits would return home. Often those who were able to return to their homes in Madagascar were recaptured and sent back to Ile de France.

It became obvious to the planters that the abolition of slavery was bound to come, no matter how much they opposed it. By 1825 the sugar industry was expanding quickly, but there were not enough slaves to work the land, and further importation had become illegal. However, the problem was partly solved when, in 1829, a group of Indian immigrants arrived on the island.

Unlike the slaves, who were not paid for their work, these indentured Indians (so-called because they were bound under contract to their masters) received five rupees every month. They also received a daily ration of rice, *dholl* (lentils) and an adequate quantity of salt, oil and mustard, although scant provision was

Indian women in their colourful saris. Their ancestors came to the island as indentured workers who were paid five rupees per month

Traditional decoration on a Hindu temple. Hinduism now has more followers than any other religion in Mauritius

made for their clothing. The agents who recruited them gave an undertaking that the immigrants would be given a free return passage to India at the end of their contract, if they chose not to renew their contracts but to become totally free again.

At first, there were many more Indian men than women in Mauritius. However, later on, the coolies (as they were called)

67

Inside a mosque. Most Mauritian Muslims belong to the Sunni group

were allowed to bring their wives and children with them. Although they came from different parts of India, belonged to different castes, spoke different languages and had many different customs, they were able to retain something of their own way of life.

Much propaganda was used to encourage Indians to go to

Mauritius to solve the labour problem. Some were even kidnapped! All heard stories that the streets in the colony were paved with gold. In addition, they were given six months' advance pay and this led them to believe that money was going to be plentiful.

Once they arrived on the island, the Indians discovered, too late, that the reality was not so attractive. Some wanted to return home when they saw the conditions under which they had to work. Indentured labour was, in fact, no more than a new system of slavery. The same masters with the same attitudes now had coolies working for them instead of slaves. The planters did not like the idea of having to pay wages. They had been used to people working for them for nothing. So they tried to make the coolies do as much as possible for their money.

The coolies could not return to India because they had signed five-year contracts. The planters who had been very happy about importing Indian coolies when the supply of slaves ran out often had to be reminded that Sunday work, unlimited hours and corporal punishment were all illegal.

The coolies were slightly better off than the slaves had been, but they were still not to be envied. Eleven per cent of them died in the first year. The government of India began to hear what the conditions in Mauritius were like and they stopped emigration to the island in May 1839. The next group of immigrants did not arrive in Mauritius until 1843.

There were tragedies connected with the coolie trade, too. One of the greatest disasters was the burning of the ship *Shah*

Jehan whilst it was bringing coolies from Calcutta to Mauritius. On June 27, 1858, a fire broke out on deck. The ship had 485 people on board. Seventy-five of them were the crew. The rest were Indian immigrants and their families. There were not enough life-boats for everyone; though rafts were made, these did not have space for sufficient food and water. In the end, only one coolie was saved.

Mauritius had been described as ''a little India with a Chinese fringe''. But it is more than that. It is a mosaic of various ethnic groups who have learned to live together in a very small country. Each community has borrowed and adopted some of the customs and habits of the others.

Languages, Religions and Cultures

Mauritius has been shaped by the influences of Asia, Europe and Africa. While preserving their original cultures, Mauritians live, work and play together, thus achieving a unity in spite of their differences.

The language most widely used in informal conversation is Creole, spoken by about ninety-five per cent of the population. Some like to describe it as a French *patois*, or dialect; others say it is a language in its own right. It was born out of the need of French-speaking masters to communicate with their slaves from Africa and Madagascar. Many of them came from Bantu tribes and, although Creole has its roots in French, Bantu has had a considerable influence on the construction of the language. It has also been affected by Indian and Chinese languages. There is, as yet, no one way of writing Creole.

According to the 1983 *Housing and Population Census of Mauritius*, there are more than twenty-two languages currently spoken on the island. Many people speak four or more. After Mauritian Creole, the language most commonly spoken is Mauritian Bhojpuri, a dialect of Hindi. This is preferred to Creole among Indo-Mauritians. Both Creole and Bhojpuri are a linguistic product of Mauritian cultural life. Bhojpuri has many Creole words.

71

Herbal remedies on sale in the market in Port Louis. Although English is the official language of Mauritius, French is widely used and is understood by nearly everyone on the island

English is still the official language of Mauritius. Nevertheless, television and radio programmes are broadcast in about a dozen languages, although the majority are in French. Even those people who may not speak and write French can understand it better than English as it is so similar to Creole.

There are only two French *lycées* (high schools) on the island. Education is based generally on the English system with children taking final school examinations set in England. Primary and secondary education are free. Mauritius has one university which runs several courses. However, those who can afford it prefer to send their children to universities abroad, particularly to Britain, France and India.

Since the Mauritian government wishes to promote linguistic harmony in this multilingual island, it encourages the learning—and the teaching in schools—of oriental languages, as well as English and French. Many Mauritians believe that the language spoken by their ancestors when they came to the island is a necesary link between their contemporary way of life and their heritage.

Another traditional element of Mauritian society is the variety of religions which exist side by side. There were over eighty religions and sects listed in the 1983 Census. The most widely followed of these are Hunduism, Christianity and Islam, in that order. There are also large numbers of adherents to the Tamil and Buddhist religions. Each of these world religions has its own practices and sacred books in which its beliefs and doctrines are enshrined.

The Hindus have many sacred books written in Sanskrit— the ancient and sacred language of India. Hinduism has not one god but many gods and goddesses, and there are a number of different Hindu sects, each with its own traditions and rituals. Temple worship is not compulsory for Hindus. Every family has a shrine at which to worship its gods and goddesses—often white or red flags are flown to show that there is a shrine in the house.

A Tamil temple in Port Louis. One of the most striking aspects of Mauritian society is the way in which so many different races and religions are able to co-exist peacefully

Christianity, in Mauritius as elsewhere, embodies belief in one God, in Jesus Christ and in the doctrines contained in the Bible. There are a number of different churches—not merely Catholic and Protestant—and Christians worship in these as they do throughout the world, particularly on Sundays.

Islam is the Arabic word meaning "submission" or "obedience" to the commands of God—known to Muslims as Allah. The sacred book of Islam is the Quran, revealed to the prophet Muhammad by the angel Gabriel. It was originally

74

The interior of a Mauritian mosque—note the traditional Islamic architecture. Islam now has more than 120,000 followers in Mauritius, making it one of the country's major religions

written in Arabic but has now been translated into many other languages. Muslims are expected to know the Quran, to understand it and to practise its teachings. They worship in mosques. Many of the Muslims in Mauritius belong to the Sunni (orthodox) group. Very few are Shias or Ahmadis, although there are some followers of these different forms of Islam.

The lives of the Indo-Mauritians in the villages are centred on the *baitka*. This is the meeting-place where the sacred scriptures are read. It is also a cultural and social centre for the

Outside a church in Curepipe. In Mauritius it is not unusual for religions to overlap—this woman may well be a Hindu and still venerate Jesus

village, and has helped people of Indian descent to retain their culture and language as well as their religion.

Similarly, the mosque and the school attached to it—the *madressah*—provide a focus for Islamic and Arabic culture, while

Hindus celebrating a religious festival at the holy lake of Grand Bassin

religious and social activities for Muslims, led by the Imam, centre on the *jammat*.

There is, of course, freedom for people of all religions to celebrate their festivals and observe their customs at all times. Muslims, for example, pray five times a day, and fast during the daylight hours of the month of Ramadan (which commemorates a journey made by Muhammad from Mecca to Medina). At the end of the month of fasting they also enjoy traditional festivities.

Of all the feasts and festivals which take place in Mauritius, the Indian ones are the most colourful and spectacular. Divali

77

The minaret of a mosque in Port Louis

(in October), for example, celebrates the victory of the hero king Rama over the demon Ravana. It is also held to honour the goddess of wealth and good fortune. Houses and buildings are decorated with lights—both electric-lamps and clay oil-lamps. These lights symbolize the victory of light over darkness. At this time, fireworks are set off to chase away the spirits of the dead, and people visit one another and exchange gifts of sweets.

A more solemn festival is the Tamil Cavadee when pilgrims walk in procession towards the temple. They usually wear yellow clothing and some of them are in a state of trance so deep that they do not feel the pain inflicted by needles and long steel spikes which are stuck into their sides, their cheeks or even their tongues. Some of the Tamil devotees even walk on hot ashes—without showing signs of being burned.

The Chinese Spring Festival or New Year falls on a different day each year because it is based on the lunar calendar. It is the custom for Chinese families to spring-clean their homes before the festival. No scissors or knives may be used on the day. Food is piled up to symbolize an abundance during the year. Crackers and fireworks are set off on the eve of the New Year to chase away evil spirits. Traditional cakes and other delicacies are distributed to relatives and friends.

There are other festivals and feasts of course, but those just described have taken on almost national status in Mauritius. However, Christmas Day remains the greatest feast of them all, celebrated by everyone. And beforehand there is a festive atmosphere all over the island, with people buying gifts for relatives and friends. Christmas falls in summer, of course—in the cyclone season. Unfortunately, now and then, it is spoilt by a cyclone.

The different cultures of the African and Malagasy slaves could not be preserved once they came to Mauritius as, not only did they originate from different tribes and parts of Africa, but they were separated on arrival. They had no choice but to adapt

A pilgrim in the Tamil Cavadee procession

Women in a Cavadee procession in Port Louis. They beat sticks together to make a rhythmic accompaniment to their progress

French culture to their needs. However, some tribal traditions still exist.

One thing which has survived is the *sega*. This is both a dance and a song. It has its roots in African and Malagasy music brought to Mauritius by the slaves. The words of the *sega* are often improvized. The modern *sega* has achieved the status of a national dance. The *ravane* (a large hoop over which a piece of goat-skin has been stretched) is really all that is needed to accompany the *sega*. However, dancers nowadays are often accompanied by a guitar and other instruments. While performing, the village dancers sometimes drink *bacco* which is prepared from rice, pineapple peelings, maize and oats, and fermented for many months in brown sugar.

One central cultural institution in Mauritius is the Mahatma Gandhi Institute which is mainly concerned with promoting oriental languages and cultures. The Institute publishes textbooks for students in primary and secondary schools, helps with the training of teachers, and organizes language, music, dance and fine arts courses.

Mauritian culture is based on a new unity—for the human history of Mauritius began only some three hundred and fifty years ago. At the same time, it is based on an ancient diversity of cultures from Europe, Africa, India and China.

Economic Development and the Future

Since the time of the British occupation of Mauritius, the economy has been based on the sugar industry. In 1835, when slave-owners were paid an indemnity for freeing their slaves, the planters had extra money available to experiment with different varieties of sugar-cane and alternative ways of producing it.

In 1853, a Chamber of Agriculture was formed. It still exists today. There, planters were able to meet and exchange ideas about improving the production of sugar. Small estates were joined to make larger ones, and the amount of sugar grown was increased.

From 1880, for various economic reasons, many large estates were divided up and the smaller plantations were sold to Indian labourers who had saved enough money to become planters. (Today small planters own about one-quarter of the country's sugar-cane fields.) Gradually, there were fewer factories but they had better equipment. The Indians grew the cane on their small plantations, the factories milled it into sugar. Even today small planters in Mauritius have their sugar milled in the big factories.

In 1922, a College of Agriculture was founded. Students, lecturers and planters worked together to continue improving the sugar output. The College of Agriculture eventually became

Spraying the sugar plants to protect them from disease. The Sugar Industry Research Institute now has an established reputation for research in improving agricultural methods

one of the three schools of the university. In 1953, the Sugar Industry Research Institute was set up. This now has a worldwide reputation. It carries out research on how to improve both the growing of sugar, and agriculture in general. It has been found that foodcrops and vegetables can successfully be grown in between rows of sugar-cane. Many experiments are

84

being carried out to see which crops grow best in this way.

By 1968, when Mauritius became independent, sugar made up ninety-three per cent of its exports. Today, Mauritius exports about 600,000 tonnes of sugar each year; about 500,000 tonnes are sold to the European Economic Community. The rest is usually sold to Canada, and the U.S.A., and to other islands in the Indian Ocean. Mauritians themselves consume about 35,000 tonnes a year.

The sugar industry employs about seventy thousand workers. Through the Sugar Industry Labour Welfare Fund, employees are loaned money to enable them to build their own concrete houses. There are also social centres where they can go to watch television, play games or borrow library books.

In the past, sugar used to be loaded on ships by dockers (many of them the descendents of slaves). In 1980, a bulk sugar terminal was built near the harbour. This has two silos, and over 175,000 tonnes of sugar can be stored in each.

Sugar has several by-products such as vinegar, perfumes, molasses, rum and many types of alcohol, all of which are produced in Mauritius. But the Mauritian government has been aware for several years that most of the island's eggs are in one basket. Mauritius is what is known as a mono-crop economy and is too dependent on sugar. The government is gradually trying to change this by encouraging the growing of different crops.

Tea is being grown more widely, particularly since it recovers from cyclones even more quickly than sugar-cane. There is also

85

wider cultivation of foodcrops and fruits so that Mauritius will be more self-sufficient in food in the near future and it will not have to import so much of what it consumes.

There are now about seventy thousand unemployed workers in Mauritius. Each year about nine thousand school-leavers come on the labour market. It is, therefore, essential to create new jobs. Since only very few can be created in the sugar industry, the government is trying to expand other sectors of the economy. There are two types of industry in Mauritius: one produces goods for the Mauritian market; the other produces goods only for export. One way in which the government

Orchids — these flowers which are native to Mauritius are a valued source of income since they are cultivated for the export market

A worker in a tea plantation. Tea is planted because it recovers from cyclones even more quickly than sugar-cane

encourages the setting up of new industries is by imposing heavy duties on imported goods, especially if similar ones are made in Mauritius. The Development Bank of Mauritius plays a major role in the export industry, by lending investors money and building factories. There are many Mauritians who participate in these industries, although a number of the industrialists come from abroad.

One of the most successful industries in Mauritius is textiles. Wool is imported from Australia and made into knitwear which is then exported for sale in supermarkets around the world. Other manufactured goods include matches, shoes, motorcycles,

A typical Mauritian harbour scene

chewing-gum, gloves, fertilizers, raincoats, poultry, balloons, furniture, toys and diamonds. The government also encourages small-scale enterprises and helps those who are willing to set up small businesses.

Tourism is the third most important industry in Mauritius. An average of ten thousand tourists arrive every month, and the Mauritius Government Tourist Board is trying to attract even more by publicizing the island abroad. Mauritius is warm all the year round. Tourists have good travel facilities and the cost of living is lower than in other islands of the Indian Ocean. Mauritius is also one of the world's most exciting places to snorkel and dive. Tourists can go deep-sea fishing around the coast. Giant marlin can be hooked quite close to the shore—indeed, the world record was established in Mauritius in 1966. Through tourism Mauritius earns foreign exchange and provides employment for many of its people.

There are some disadvantages as a result of tourism, of course. Seafood, such as crab, lobster and oysters, is sold to the hotels for visitors and tends to become too expensive for most Mauritians to buy. Also, some of the hotels are owned by

A giant marlin. Deep-sea fishing is popular with Mauritians and with tourists

One of Mauritius' beautiful beaches—a major tourist attraction

foreigners which means that any profits go out of the country.

There are still many poor people in Mauritius who do not have enough food or clothing, and who live in tin shacks. Many still cannot afford to have electricity in their homes. However, the government is trying very hard to solve the problems of the poor, many of which arise because of over-population. Mauritius is one of the most densely populated countries in the world. The government is succeeding in its campaign to persuade Mauritians to have smaller families but there will still be too many people in Mauritius for a very long time to come. Meanwhile, heads of families who are unemployed receive some

There are many poor people in Mauritius — often with homes like this

money every month to make sure their families do not starve. There are also family allowances, old-age pensions and free medical services. Rice and flour, the basic foods of Mauritians, are subsidized by the government.

The government is also heavily committed to education. Primary and secondary education are free, and there are some free pre-primary nursery schools. The government broadcasts educational programmes and is doing its best to establish a national network of libraries both in urban and rural areas.

Mauritius is one of the few countries which has a Minister for Women's Affairs and Family Welfare. Her Ministry looks after the interests of Mauritian women who have always contributed a great deal to the development of the country. Some continue to work in the fields side by side with men. Others work as teachers, nurses, accountants, doctors and lawyers. Many are now working in factories. Very often a women is the only breadwinner in a large family, for many of the factories prefer female to male labour. Many, of course, stay at home, as women all over the world have done for centuries. They, too, contribute to the development of the nation by making sure that families are well looked after, properly fed and happy.

There is every hope that in the near future every Mauritian will be able to earn a good livelihood with the help of an enlightened and democratic government.

Index